# Willows & Wings

## Inspirational Poems
by
LaVonne Puha

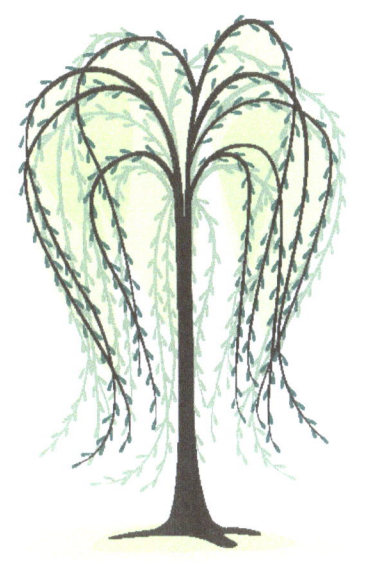

# Willows & Wings
Inspirational Poems
by
LaVonne Puha

Devine Inspiration Book Publishers

Book Design by Patty Atcheson-Melton

Copyright © 2013, By Lavonne Puha
All rights reserved, including the right of reproduction
in whole or in part in any form.

Puha, LaVonne
1. Poetry  2. Religious

This book contains material protected under
International and Federal Copyright Laws and Treaties.
Any unauthorized reprint or use of this material
is prohibited, under civil and
federal and governmental penalties.

ISBN: 978-0-9896210-0-7

# Dedication

I dedicate my first book of poetry to my Lord Jesus, who gave me the inspiration to put my thoughts down on paper, and the opportunity to share them with others.

To my husband Warren, and my sons, Jerrid, Jake, Josiah, and Justin Puha, who have always believed in me, and I now have a legacy to leave them.

To my mother and father for giving me life, and always doing outdoor activities, and keeping us close to nature.

# Acknowledgements

To my parents, Don and Jean Henriks for encouraging the creative side of me, and for raising me in the country in several states, where I was exposed to many different types of nature. They allowed me to have everything from horses, to raccoons and wolf pups.

To my family who have always believed in me, and inspired me. Just our family times alone inspired many of my writings. To my Faith Arena family for wonderful teachings on God's word, and for encouraging me to be and do what God has called me too.

To Patty Melton for making this all come together. I'm thankful to have met her.

# Contents

*The Great Willow...13*

*You Are My Delight...15*

*The Onlu One I See...17*

*Hidden Dreams...19*

*Dare To Believe...21*

*The Glory...23*

*Put The Petal To The Metal...25*

*Times With God...27*

*I Am...29*

*It's all About You...31*

*One Standing...33*

*Wisdom Calling...35*

*Fining Wisdom...37*

*Oh Lord...39*

*Learning To Rest...41*

*Resting In The Lord...43*

*That Kind Of God...45*

*You Are My Life...47*

*Think Of Me...49*

*Gods Peace...51*

*Laughter...35*

*Joy...55*

*Lord You Are...57*

*Forgiveness...59*

*God Is There...61*

*Eyes Of Faith...62*

*Tear Drops...65*

*Giving...66*

*Hurting Heart...69*

*Enjoy Life...71*

*The Wind And Me...72*

*The Ocean, God, And Me...75*

*Hawaiian Sunrise...77*

*Silent Stars...79*

*Reflection Of Life...81*

*Sweet Sunshine...83*

*Shade Tree...84*

*My Mother...86*

*Our Beloved Dad...88*

*Our Sons...91*

*Woman Of God...93*

*Eyes Of My Heart...94*

*Father Cradle Me...97*

*Forever IN Love With YOU...99*

*Lord You're My Lifeline...100*

*God's Plan...102*

*Spiritual Journey...105*

*Loves Whispered Song...107*

*Me And You...109*

*Once In A Lifetime Love...111*

*America...113*

*About The Author...115*

# The Great Willow

*There was a Great Willow and a man.*
*This man looked up with weary eyes*
*The Great Willow reached down to take his hand*
*He rested in the Great Willows arms*
*Until the end of day*
*With strength renewed, and faith restored*
*He could now see his way*
*The Great Willow gently put him down*
*As like a gentle breeze*
*With eyes now open, he looked up*
*Then fell on bended knees.*

# You Are My Delight

*I created all with let there be*
*The sun, the moon, and the stars you see*
*Every leaf on every tree*
*Every flower in the breeze*
*When I look into the Crystal Sea*
*Your reflection is what I see*
*My heart desired a family*
*That is why I created thee*
*You are my delight child, you are my delight*
*You are the apple of my eye*
*You are my delight.*
*I created all with Let There Be*
*From the deepest ocean*
*To the highest mountain peak*
*Every blade of grass as far as the eye can see*
*I created all with let there be*
*I created you child, I created you for me*
*You are my delight child, you are my delight*
*When I look at you, I see me.*

# The Only One I See

*The only one I see*
*Is the only one I dare believe*
*For in this world of wickedness*
*He lifts me up and gives me rest*

*I know that I can count on him*
*For unlike me he is not a man*
*Because of this he cannot lie*
*And on this truth I do rely*

*He promised he would never leave*
*But guide me everyday*
*To always walk beside me*
*In his loving gentle way*

*At times he just might carry me*
*But stop..... We never will*
*Faithful is the one I see*
*The only one I dare believe*

# Hidden Dreams

*I will no longer search for hidden dreams*
*Tucked way down deep where no one sees*
*Deep in your mind starts a thought to unfold*
*Deep thoughts quietly listening*
*Yet still these thoughts go untold*
*There are things deep inside of you to be done*
*Books to be written, songs to be sung*
*No one will ever see the things you see*
*No one will ever hear the things you hear*
*If you don't get up, and light a fire beneath you*
*And do something about it.*
*Prosperity waits for no one*
*You have to take hold and seize it for yourself*
*Knowing that the one who gave you these inspired ideas*
*Is standing right there with you*
*The Great I Am, the Lord himself.*

# Dare To Believe

*It takes Faith to believe*
*I'm beginning to see*
*Where the Lord leads*
*I must follow*

*God won't take his hand off me*
*But show me the way*
*For he cares for me*
*I must only believe*

*Even when I can't see*
*He'll take every care*
*He'll take every need*
*And cast them all far from me*

*My part..... Only Believe.*

# The Glory of the Lord

*I've seen the Glory of the Lord*
*As I watch him work his plan for me*
*As waves that thunder against the cliffs*
*So is the voice of the Lord*

*As a wind blowing through the palm trees*
*So is the Lord whispering his love for me*

*As a flower gently swaying in the breeze*
*So is the Lords hand gently guiding me*

*As the mountains stand majestic and high*
*So is the Lords power and might*

*As a river runs pure and sweet*
*So are the living waters flowing out of me*

*Yes, I've seen the Glory of the Lord*
*As I watch him work his plan for me.*

# Put The Petal To The Metal

*Why do I think of days gone by*
*So many yesterday's gone with the wind*
*Nothing can change the past*
*Only the present, and the future*
*Can be dreams lived, and realities made true*
*To think in the past will leave you at a stand still*
*You can't go back, you are afraid to go ahead*
*Afraid to make the same mistakes*
*Or maybe your past was so great you want to live it again*
*Either way you need to get past this place of idle movement*
*Put the petal of faith to the metal of hope*
*And race away on the wings of life*
*You don't always have to know what lies ahead.*

# Times With God

*It's those special times Lord that I love you so*
*Those times when it's just you and me that mean the most*
*I lift up Holy hands, to you I sing*
*I dance around, worshiping my King*
*I close my eyes, keeping the world out*
*This is our time together*
*Our time to shout*
*Uninhibited praise fills the atmosphere*
*I think even the angles rejoice over the time we share*
*There is nothing more real, nothing more true*
*Than to know that the King of all existence*
*Has been laughing with you.*

# I Am

I am a majestic mountain
My name is wisdom
I am the sun shining bright, warming the earth
My name is nurturing
I am a rippling stream
My name is joy unspeakable
I am the great ocean blue
My name is excellence
I am a full moon lighting up a quiet night
My name is peace
I am the stars sparkling in all their brilliance
My name is faith
I am an exquisite rainbow; a promise stretched out across the sky
My name is integrity
I am a meadow carpeted in a tapestry of colors
My name is gentleness
I am a breathtaking brilliant sunset
My name is hope
I am the Lord your God
My name is love.

# It's All About You

*Sitting in the early morning*
*So quiet, peaceful, and serine,*
*I smile at my tender thoughts*
*It's all about you*
*Walking through a spring meadow*
*A carpet of wildflowers blooming*
*Their sweet smell filling my senses*
*It's all about you*
*Looking up at the majestic mountains*
*Standing strong, proud, and tall,*
*It's all about you*
*Walking along a forest trail*
*The natural beauty that's been created*
*Breathing in tranquility*
*It's all about you*
*Every thought I've ever had, every dream I've ever dreamed*
*Each and every wondrous day I live*
*It's all about you Lord; It's all about you.*

# One Standing

*When I hear the mighty sound of thunder*
*It makes me think this is how God speaks to my enemy*
*Forcing it away from me*
*When I see lightning strike*
*It feels like God's warning all*
*Not to mess with his child*
*The one he has called.*
*The force of wind that blows*
*Takes every weight and care from me*
*Throwing it all far from me…into infinity.*
*The strong in the Lord stand like a mighty oak tree*
*Bending with the storms of life*
*Never giving up or breaking; the faithful ones still hold their ground*
*After a heavy rain, the righteous are like seed planted in good ground*
*That can't be washed away*
*The calmness of all who have maintained their stance*
*Are the ones who will be around in the last… of the last days*
*Still standing proud through life's ups and downs*
*Knowing full well where they get their strength.*
*These are the ones who have learned to rest in God*
*Living daily in Gods wisdom, righteousness, and grace.*

# Wisdom Calling

*Can you hear me calling*
*I'm calling after you*
*Take the time to listen*
*My words are powerful, yet few*

*Close your eyes, take a breath*
*Listen with your heart*
*Wisdom's lessons never end*
*So come my child, let's start*

*I'll take it very slowly*
*So you learn to meditate*
*On every word you hear from God*
*Learning to rest in his loving Grace*

*Your life is only as good as you speak out*
*So speak out loud and clear*
*All things you want to come true*
*In faith, and boldness*
*Speak to the atmosphere.*

# Finding Wisdom

*I hear you, I must find you*
*I look for you, I must see*
*In the distance I know you're calling*
*Come close, come close to me*

*In my heart I feel a tugging*
*A yearning from inside*
*I want to walk beside you*
*yes closely by your side*

*With newfound understanding*
*My life will surely change*
*Yes, I know you now*
*Wisdom is your name.*

## Oh Lord

*Lord, you said to follow you*
*And you'd always see me through*
*I said I trusted you Oh Lord*
*And I'll continue too*

*You said you'd always love me*
*This you've proved is true*
*Oh Lord, what did I ever do*
*To deserve a love such as you?*

# Learning To Rest

*Life was passing me by*
*So many cares seem to come with this life*
*Holding on to simple things seemed to take such time*
*The simple things I loved*
*Were harder and harder to find*
*Demands on myself day after day*
*Became trying on my very being*
*I had to find another way.*
*Then I met you Lord*
*And you set my soul free*
*You taught me how to rest in you*
*For a life of liberty.*

# Resting In The Lord

*I am the only one you need my child*
*Take my hand and follow me*
*For I will show you how to live your life*
*Being the best that you can be*
*The is no struggle to achieve the very best*
*Learn to trust in me, learn to be at rest*
*I don't take things fast*
*Nor do I take them slow*
*For when you're in the will of God*
*Things just seem to flow*
*Many pleasures in life will tempt you*
*All the glimmer, all the glow*
*Watch out for worldly treasures*
*One day they'll have to go*
*Instead, look to me*
*Righteous and true*
*And know that's how I see you child*
*When I look at you.*

# That Kind Of God

*You're just that kind of God*
*Who sees the best in me*
*You're just that kind of God*
*Who likes the victory*
*You're just that kind of God*
*Who loves to give me zeal*
*You're just that kind of God*
*Who loves to see me healed*
*You're just that kind of God*
*Who loves to laugh with me*
*You're just that kind of God*
*Who loves to see me free*
*You're just that kind of God*
*Who walks right next to me*
*You're just that kind of God*
*Who sees righteousness in me*
*You're just that kind of God*
*I'll follow every day*
*You're just that kind of God*
*Who will always show me the way.*

# You Are My Life

*I long to be close to you*
*Knowing you, and to be known by you*
*Your words are pure life to me*
*Sustains me through each and every day*
*I walk straight ahead*
*I will not crawl*
*You keep me lifted up*
*Therefore I will never fall*
*You say stop, I stop*
*You say walk, I walk*
*You say stand, I stand*
*You say follow me…*
*I'm already there.*

# Think Of Me

*When you see a brilliant rainbow stretched across the sky*
*Or birds singing sweet melodies as they pass by*
*Think of me*
*The next time you see the sunrise on a brand new day*
*The morning dew glistening on a tender leaf, before it fades away*
*Think of me*
*When you see a majestic mountain standing tall*
*An eagle flying bold and strong*
*Think of me*
*The next time you hear the thunder on a stormy day*
*As you see the sky turn from blue to grey*
*Think of me*
*When you see a meadow so green*
*With a blanket of wildflowers blowing in the breeze*
*Think of me*
*The next time you listen to the wind gain intensity*
*As you close your eyes letting the rain sooth your cares away*
*Think of me*
*When you ask yourself the question, is there a love so deep*
*That someone would lay down their life for another human being*
*Think of me.*

# Gods Peace

As I float weightlessly in a tide pool
Graceful, and with calm ease
I recognize this feeling now
It's Gods peace that surpasses all understanding
A precious gift he gave to me

A soothing in my heart that brings a smile to my face
A calm feeling so wonderful
I bath in its embrace

Taking a deep breath washes every care away
I close my eyes and listen to all the beautiful sounds
That surrounds my world, my space
So thankful for Gods loving peace
And for his loving Grace.

# Laughter

*Laughter is like a medicine*
*You need it everyday*
*For it will heal a broken body*
*From inside out, laughter's healing has her way*
*Laughter doesn't take anything for granted*
*Doesn't live on yesterday*
*It makes every day count*
*It builds up somehow, someway*
*You can't stop laughter from happening*
*It's just like the sun and the sky*
*It rises up to another beautiful day*
*Flows out from deep inside*
*Once the ball starts rolling, there's no slowing down.*
*Although some like to think*
*They can get by with just a smile*
*Are kidding themselves*
*And I'll tell you how*
*God intended it to mean much more in your life*
*When God laughs, he laughs out loud.*

# *Joy*

*Joy unspeakable, joy that's reachable*
*Is available to all who seek it*
*You can buy things for yourself*
*Or buy things for others that bring you joy*
*But you can't buy joy itself*
*You can't lend yours out*
*You can't borrow some from others*
*You can't pay one price to live in it everyday*
*Or keep hold of it forever*
*The only way to get joy is to receive it*
*As a gift from God*
*Then learn to walk in that joy*
*God wants you to live a joyful life*
*After all, he did send his son to pay the price for exactly that.*

# Lord You Are

*Lord, you are my sunshine*
*You are everything bright in my life*
*You cause me to grow in your penetrating light*
*Lord you are my oak tree*
*Sturdy and strong*
*I look to you each day*
*To help me stay strong*
*Lord you are my eagle*
*Seeing things before me*
*Guiding me through life*
*With your wisdom and truth*
*Lord you are my meadow*
*When I seek peace, I rest in you*
*Like wildflowers, you are every color of the rainbow*
*You are every dream come true*
*Lord you are my mighty river*
*Raging onwards towards the future*
*There is no going back*
*As a river flows, so does one's life.*

# Forgiveness

*Forgiveness is such a wonderful gift*
*Everyone at one time or another has needed it*
*There are no age limits or racial discriminations*
*when it comes to forgiveness*
*Just one heart truly crying out for it*
*And one heart releasing that forgiveness*
*When people can learn to love one another*
*and to be forgiving*
*The way the Lord has forgiven us*
*Then this world has a chance.*

# God Is There

*In your darkest despairs*
*God is the one waiting there*
*To lift you back up to the Son*
*By his side, where you belong*
*Learn from the trails that you go through*
*Gain strength and character with each day new*
*Keep your eyes on God above*
*For nothing you've done can stop his love.*

# Eyes Of Faith

*Can you see the Lord*
*In everything you do and see*
*Look through eyes of faith*
*As you go about your day*

*Can you see him in the icicles*
*Hanging from the roof*
*Reminds me of the sword of faith*
*Piercing words of truth*

*Can you see him in the snow glistening like diamonds*
*On a bright sunny winters day*
*Or in the snowman being created*
*By children as they play*
*Can you see him in the clouds*
*As sunset falls to night*
*Or in the cry of a wolf*
*On the same bright moonlit night*

*Can you see him on a winter's day*
*When snowflakes fall gently to the ground*
*Or in a graceful deer*
*As she walks without a sound*

*Can you see him in a glorious sunrise*
*Over the mountaintops so high*
*Or in a beautiful rainbow*
*His promises, stretched across the sky*

*Can you see the Lord*
*In everything you do and see*
*Look through eyes of faith*
*As you go about your day.*

# Tear Drops

*Tears can flow from wounded eyes*
*Like rivers down ones cheek*
*The ache in a heart can hurt so much*
*That it makes it hard to breath*
*Some tears make you want to cry out…*
*LORD HELP, into the atmosphere*
*Some tears make you fall to your knees*
*Quiet whispers only the Lord can hear*
*Then there are some tears that are joyful*
*Coming from happy times you've known*
*And some are from a love inside*
*For someone that you know*
*Different tears mean different things*
*Sometimes they need to flow*
*For that's Gods way of showing you*
*They help to cleanse your soul.*

# Giving

*Giving is a quality that comes from the heart*

*It's a gift Gods given us*

*To partake of, then pass on to someone else*

*There is no feeling in the world that makes you feel so exhilarant*

*Than the feeling you get after God has blessed you*

*And then turn around and become someone else's blessing*

*And help them capture their dreams.*

*Giving is an expression of love*

*And since God is all love*

*We know we are doing his divine calling*
*When you give whole-heartedly to someone*
*A feeling of excitement explodes inside of you*
*When you see the hope and faith come alive in them*
*When they partake of this wonderful act of giving*
*That someone has freely laid before them*
*And see what a truly wonderful God we serve*
*Doing his amazing acts of love through each person*
*They too can't help but wait expectantly*
*For someone to impart this electrifying experience of love to*
*That a good God has brought about*
*When they do, the whole process starts again.*
*Can you imagine the impact we as Christians*
*could have on this earth*
*If we all tapped into this gift of giving that Gods given us*
*Directed it to others with zeal!*
*This planet would explode with the revelation*
*Of walking in, and living as the truly elite*
*The righteousness of God*
*Living in his grace*
*Praising, worshiping, and resting in*
*A truly Big, and Good, Good, God.*

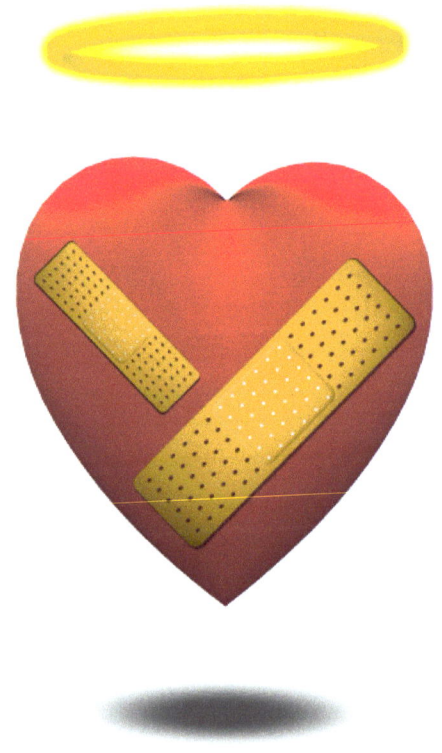

# Hurting Heart

*Why do I feel this way?*
*My heart is hurting, yet I can't get away*

*It seems to me that things should change*
*Nobody hears me, although I scream*

*Is my pain inside so deep they don't see*
*Or is no one listening, just looking past me*

*What do I do to get the attention of someone*
*I've tried to cry out, I've tried to run*

*Oh Lord, hear my cry, answer my prayers*
*Please send me someone in my life that cares.*

# Enjoy Life

*Sometimes it surprises me when there has been beauty all around me*
*But somehow I didn't see.*
*I got so caught up in all of life's challenges*
*That I missed what was right in front of me*

*Then one day I woke up, and thought to myself,*
*"What was I thinking," life is good, and right here for the taking!*
*After all, I've never seen a sunset that didn't make me sigh*
*Or witnessed a sunrise with such beauty*

*Oh, what was I thinking to let these God given moments pass by*
*Without a gratefulness in my heart*
*To thank him for his magnificence*

*When it starts to rain on a hot summer's day*
*And clouds roll in with thunder, and lightning strikes across the sky*
*The horses start to run, buck, and play*
*Even they know how to appreciate a day*

*How about after the rain, when everything smells so fresh and sweet*
*Or looking at the brilliant rainbow stretched out over the sky*
*As far as the eye can see*

*Little frogs croak their songs, while birds sing in harmony*
*Have you ever heard such wonders*
*Coming from mouths as small as these*

*So every day, learn to appreciate*
*The big things and the small*
*For life goes on either way*
*You want to be a part of it, after al!*

# The Wind And Me

*Wind, come away with me*
*We'll fly so high through the bright sunny sky*
*As we pass by a cloud, I'll let you drop me down*
*Ever so softly in the middle of one of these beautiful*
*Heavenly, white puffs of pleasure*

*What joy it is to sit in the clouds as you gracefully glide me*
*Across the brilliant blue sky*
*I see many wonderful things in these pillows of white loveliness*
*One is the shape of a cute little lamb, another*
*like a boy and his dog*

*Another is like a sailboat passing by so carefree*
*Oh wind, what wonders I see when I let the Holy Spirit flow free*
*Blow me now wind over the water's edge*
*See how the water and sun work together to give life*
*to Gods wonderful creations*
*The trees with their roots so deep in the earth*
*Reaching toward the cool refreshing nourishment it seeks*
*Reminds me of myself, thirsting after the things of God*
*The flowers soaking up the warmth of the sun*
*Thrives and grows as a person does on every word of God*
*Go now wind, across the water ever so gently,*
*as not to miss a thing*
*As the sunlight dances on the water like diamonds*
*I watch this glistening wonder, and relax into a dreamlike state*
*So close to nature, so close to my Lord*
*Which to me are one in the same*
*I can clearly hear what the Lord has to tell me*
*We laugh, we sing, we capture yet another*
*wonderful time together*
*Here in this pure untouched nature*
*The Holy Spirit whispers to me as the breeze*
*And I close my eyes, take a deep breath*
*And relax in his comfort*
*Oh wind, what a time we've had enjoying this gift of imagination*
*Freely giving, freely living, and to some, freely reality.*

# The Ocean, God, and Me

*Looking at the ocean, what a wondrous sight*
*Sitting on the rocks after the tides gone out*
*Are the special times I spend with the Lord*
*Every care is washed from my mind*

*Looking down into the tide pools*
*Sea life has been captured for me to explore*
*I swim in this pool Gods made for me*
*All this beauty some don't know of*
*That's living underneath, waiting to be explored*
*Surely one of Gods best works of faith*
*A rainbow of color for your eyes to see*

*He is the artist, the earth his canvas*
*The paintbrush his word*
*Painting existence as he spoke out*
*Let there be, Let there be.*

# Hawaiian Sunrise

*The splendor of a sunrise*
*On a cool Hawaiian mourn*
*Let's me see the awesome things*
*Our God above has done*
*As the sun comes up to greet us*
*And lays a kiss upon the earth*
*All of life awakens*
*Drinking in its nourishment*
*The quiet of the moment*
*Is soothing to the soul*
*The sun glistening on the water*
*Has a mystic glow*
*Flowers start to open, birds start to sing*
*Praising God in their own way*
*For creating everything.*

# Silent Stars

Silent stars up in the sky
Sparkling like diamonds in the night
You radiate love without even trying
An awesome creation, a wondrous sight

Silent stars up in the sky
So quiet, yet so bold
Take over the night with your dance of delight
You are truly a glorious sight

Silent stars up in the sky
God's special Christmas lights
Stung across the sky so bright
I look upon your beauty each night

Silent stars up in the sky
Stretched out as a blanket of light
I stand in awe with sheer delight
Oh how I love silent stars at night.

# Reflections of Life

*The ocean reminds me of myself*
*Tossing in the wind*
*Crashing hard into the rocks*
*Then pulled back out again*
*As the ocean is with all its depth*
*My feelings too run deep*
*Why does it seem so hard for some*
*To see this side of me*
*I want to reach inside myself*
*And find what's real to me*
*There's more to me than meets the eye*
*I have passions, hopes, and dreams*
*At times this current of life*
*Turns me upside down*
*I have to fight with all I've got*
*To get my feet back on the ground*
*But fight is just what I will do*
*With strength that is within*
*For giving up is not a choice*
*I have a new day to begin.*

## Sweet Sunshine

*The sun is shining down on me*
*Its warmth sooths my soul*
*Oh sun, do you realize how deep you reach inside of me*
*Causing me, like all life, to grow*

*You awaken and revive all my senses*
*This warmth that flows from head to toe*
*I can close my eyes, take a breath, and relax*
*Letting your radiant energy flow*

*Each ray of your sunshine has a path to follow*
*As it disperses its warmth on the earth below*
*On your journey to sustain life, sweet sunshine*
*Thank you for soothing my soul.*

# Shade Tree

*Shade tree, how I love to sit beneath your large branches*
*I can lie down on my back, and look up at you*
*Feeling nothing but peaceful feelings running through my veins*
*As I look up at you I see a birds nest*
*With tiny birds nesting in it*

*The mother and father are busy getting food for the babies*
*And seem quite content in their home*
*You have allowed them to build in your branches.*
*A squirrel is running up your trunk with acorns in her mouth*
*She is collecting for winter.*
*She also has a home here among your thick branches*
*As I continue to watch all of this activity,*
*I notice a spider off to one side*
*I never really looked close at a spider web before*
*But I find it very detailed, with interesting shapes*
*Every part spun so delicately*
*I have come to the conclusion shade tree*
*That God wonderfully made you*
*He saw you not only as a pleasant way to shade the earth,*
*and its people*
*But also as a solid, firm, safe dwelling*
*For many of his other creations*
*I to will look upon you in a different way*
*You've brought such joy to so many in a single day*
*..What memories you must have, oh tree of ancient days.*

# *My Mother*

*Mother, you've always been there for me*
*I don't know what I would have done without you*

*I started being your daughter in your womb*
*God gave me life through you; I was part of your very being*
*And you carried me through*
*You fought for me then*

*And I know you'll fight for me till the end*

*How did you know just when to laugh, and when to cry*
*Some days all I wanted to do was just pass you by*
*But you always seemed to know what was going on with me*
*And in your special way, you saw right through me*

*You've helped me grow through the years*
*You said growing took time, laughter, and tears*
*You always said to be the best that I could be*
*And only except the best that life had to offer me*

*In tough times I try to remember all that you've taught me*
*And If I had just one wish come true*
*It would be for someone to tell me, that I was just like you*
*Since I was a little girl you've wiped every tear*
*And kissed every skinned knee*
*Today, though I'm older, you still wipe the tears away*

*I can't imagine my life without you in it*
*The best part of me, I get from you*
*I believe when God thought of how a mother should be*
*He wrapped all the qualities you have together*
*And with his mighty words said*
*Let There Be*

# Our Beloved Dad

Beloved dad, you're a very special man in so many ways
You always took life so kicked back
A good western made your day

Always ready with a joke
A deck of cards in hand
Sitting at the kitchen table
Listening to a country band

You had a sense of humor
More stories than we could count
The laughter we've shared over the years
Is timeless, never to run out

*You were the most honest man we ever knew*
*A lie you would not tell*
*Never spoke an unkind word*
*Everyone you treated well*

*Each time we look up at the sky,*
*Reminds us all of you*
*For dad, you had the most beautiful eyes*
*The color of sky blue*

*Our beloved dad, our precious dad*
*We hold you always near*
*The love you've shown to each of us*
*Is a love we'll cherish, and hold dear*

*Our hearts are filled with memories*
*We'll always hold onto*
*Though tears will fall, quite normal after all*
*When you love someone has much as we have you*

*So dad, you've found a wonderful place*
*A place you've chosen to stay*
*And though we miss you very much*
*We know in our hearts*

*We'll see you again one day.*

# Our Sons

*Son, you're the apple of our eye*
*To watch you grow has been the best thing in our lives*
*From a boy, to a mighty man of God*
*We'll always be proud of you*

*Living without you is something I know we couldn't do*
*You are the very best part of us*
*I hope we're the best part of you*
*For you, there's nothing we wouldn't do*

*We've tried our best to be all the things you've needed us to be*
*From laughs, hugs, and kisses*
*To tears of growing pains*
*And a kiss on a skinned knee*

*We believe when God thought of how a son should be*
*He wrapped all the qualities you have together*
*And with his mighty words said*
*Let There BE*

# Woman Of God

*Woman of God I commend you*
*For your steadfast faith*
*Your loving kindness, gentle grace*

*Woman of God I know you*
*A delicate flower in the rain*
*A silent, radiant beauty*
*A peaceful, fragrant friend*

*Woman of God I think of you*
*As an eagle soaring in the wind*
*A kind of unleashed freedom*
*An awesome new life to begin*

*Woman of God I see you*
*Each night I step out the door*
*In a bright and shining star*
*So close, and yet so far*

*Woman of God I hear you*
*In the grandstands far above*
*Cheering each of us on*
*To finish the race that we've begun*

*Woman of God you weren't taken from us*
*But it was your will and yours alone*
*When you decided that you'd finished your race*
*And it was time*
*For you*
*To go home.*

# Eyes of My Heart

*When I think of you*
*As I often do*
*I think of a flourishing flower*
*A beauty to unfold*
*A boldness of its own*

*This I see through the eyes of my heart*

*When I think of you*
*As I often do*
*I think of a rippling stream*
*Still waters that run deep*
*A wisdom that I seek*

*This I see through the eyes of my heart*

*When I think of you*
*As I often do*
*I think of a springtime rain*
*Gently speaks to me*
*As it waters a seed in me*

*This I see through the eyes of my heart*

*You're this and so much more*
*A purity I adore*
*I'm so thankful to my Lord and King*
*For today he so blessed me*
*By allowing me to see*

*How he see you through the eyes of his heart*

# Father Cradle Me

*Father, cradle me in your loving arms*
*Rock me like a child*
*Sooth me with your tender voice*
*Speak your truths out loud*

*Shelter me beneath your mighty wings*
*Keep me from all harm*
*I know I'm safe, and can be at rest*
*Cradled in your loving arms*

*Father, teach me about love and hope*
*Teach me about faith*
*Give me understanding, and wisdom*
*To walk in every day.*

# Forever In Love With You

Take me by the hand, let's fly away
Like an eagle soaring high
To a distant land
Let your word embrace me
Let your peace, and grace surround me
I will forever be in love with you

Let us walk together day and night
I see you gentle as a dove
Yet full of might
Help me learn to love you boldly
Speak your words of truth
I will forever be in love with you

Take me by the hand, dance with me
So graceful and so lovely
Like a gentle breeze
I only want to be true to you
Serve you my whole life through
I will forever be in love with you.

# Lord You're My Lifeline

*Lord you're my lifeline*
*Simple and true*
*Each day I surrender*
*My own will to you*

*Such great love was shown*
*Giving your life on that day*
*Now I give mine to you*
*Proclaiming you are the way*

*I trust you completely*
*Believe what you say*
*Stand my ground strongly*
*Refusing to sway*

*Your words are pure life*
*Your truths are profound*
*Showing me daily*
*Steadfast love does abound*

*My worship I lift up*
*Dance, praise, and sing*
*Boldly I call out*
*You are my king*

*Humbly I bow down*
*I call out your name*
*Without a doubt knowing*
*You'll stay always the same*

*You've bathed me in truth*
*Cleansed all sin away*
*I lift Holy hands*
*Receiving grace each new day*

*Your peace I receive*
*Each day fresh and new*
*Lord you're my lifeline*
*Simple and true.*

# God's Plan

*I hear a whisper in my ear*
*That's very clear to me*
*The Holy Spirit calling softly*
*Come, I'll set you free*

*I want to tell you of Gods plan*
*In your life and family*
*The plans he has to prosper you*
*A life of victory*

*I want to show you all of his blessings*
*Bestowed on you each day*
*Grace, mercy, joy, hope, and love*
*Are just a few he freely gave*

*You have an inheritance that's yours to keep*
*Stick with me and listen well*
*I'll teach you through wisdom and grace*
*How to take hold of these, my child*

*When God gave, he gave his best*
*Because he saw the end*
*That he in turn would reap the best*
*That's where you, my child, come in.*

# Spiritual Journey

*You're the captain of this ship*
*Taking us on a spiritual journey*
*The words you preach to us, feeds us*
*The love you show us, comforts us*

*When the storms of life arise*
*The words of wisdom you've taught us will suffice*
*When the winds all cease to blow*
*The peace of God does flow*

*On that day you stand before the King*
*I believe with love filled eyes he'll say*
*Well done, my good and faithful servant*
*You've been faithful in all things.*

# Loves Whispered Song

*This union you have formed*
*Pure as two white doves, to each you now belong*
*Will stand against all storms*
*Singing loves whispered song*

*Entwined in each other's arms*
*Gods hand of grace on you*
*A three stranded cord not quickly broken*
*Every dream he'll make come true*

*Tender moments bring tender memories*
*Capture them, and keep them safe*
*Embrace them in your heart of hearts*
*Enclose them in your secret hiding place*

*As you start this blissful journey*
*Two hearts that have waited for so long*
*Like morning dew glistening in the sun*
*Will dance to loves whispered song.*

# Me And You

*I give you the best of me*
*Everything I am, is everything you see*
*From one day to the next, I'll stay the same*
*You'll never see a drastic change*

*There will be no surprises behind a hidden mood*
*All will be open, nothing misconstrued*
*I will always be honest, I'll always be true*
*My lips will always speak uplifting words to you*

*The tranquility of two hearts*
*Wrapped around each other in love*
*Will surely outdo the millions of stars above*

*I'm truly thankful to God it's true*
*For hearing my prayers*
*Then answering them too*
*Which united me, my love, with you.*

# Once In A Lifetime Love

*I sit and think of the love you once knew*
*Only to find that looking at you only confirms*
*That a once in a lifetime love is so hard to come by*
*And one you should do everything possible to hang on to*

*If you should ever loose such a love as this*
*It might walk out of your lives for good*
*And reclaiming it will not be as easy*
*As the first time you found each other*

*If you ever have a chance to reclaim*
*This once in a lifetime love, do so*
*For God sometimes opens the door a second time*
*But it's up to you, to walk through it.*

# *America*

*My home is so far away*
*The longing in my heart grows strong*
*To see the ones I love, and see their faces*
*As I walk this long road home*
*I can still see them in the distance*
*Their prayers follow me wherever I go*
*God's blessing is on America*
*Therefore his hand is on me*

*The covenant God made with Abraham*
*Was made stronger through the blood of*
*Jesus for today*
*Nobody, nowhere, no how, no way*
*Can take this great land, America away*
*For it will always stay*
*Land of the free, home of the brave.*

# About the Author

LaVonne was born in San Diego, California, and although she moved with her family several times, Oregon and Alaska is where she called home. She now resides on the island of Maui, Hawaii.

She met her Hawaiian husband while on vacation in Honolulu in 1979 and they have four beautiful sons. Although they moved away for over twenty years, the ocean drew them back. LaVonne and her family love to go snorkeling to visit her friends the turtles. She loves fishing, camping, barbeques on the beach, and whale watching, where she says the whales live her life, six months in Alaska, six months in Hawaii.

She has also experienced different cultures. The Hawaiian culture, the Alaskan culture, and the Southern culture, as they lived twelve years in Laurel, Mississippi.

LaVonne says there is beauty and peace everywhere, if you just listen. Nature has a lot to say if you just look around with an open heart, and hearing ears.

www.ingramcontent.com/pod-product-compliance
Lightning Source LLC
Chambersburg PA
CBHW042336150426
43195CB00001B/11